MW01245816

Nicole E Wicks

Can You Hear Me
~~SCREAMING~~ Knocking?

CAN YOU HEAR ME SCREAMING?

Written by Nicole E Wicks

Published by Nicole E Wicks

Copyright © 2024 by Nicole E Wicks. All rights reserved. No portion of this book may be used in any form without written permission of the publisher, with the exception of brief excerpts in articles and reviews.

ISBN-13 (paperback): 979-8-218-45805-8

Cover art by Zion Smith

Cover design by Nicole E Wicks

To my girls, my best friends, thank you for holding my
hand every time I got lost in my own mind.
I love you.

Forward

I've known Nicole for quite some time now. I can say with all conviction that she is a true artist. She speaks on things that may seem taboo for Christians to discuss. Nicole is so unapologetically herself because she knows where the gift comes from and realizes that such a gift will bring equalized hatred. The truth dealers are a rare bunch and she is among those that will speak the truth no matter what. All I ask is that you come into this collection with an open mind, open heart, and an open soul.

Leave religion at the door because it has no place here. The themes she explores will be hard for some to read or you'll feel like you're finally being heard. This is what the world is missing… truth. It's been missing people who are so spiritually connected not just with God but with people and everything around them. People who feel so intently and intensely.

I am very proud of Nicole for airing out what's inside of her, she may not realize it yet but this collection will be someone's answered prayer. This collection is proof that whatever you're going through now, shall pass. The pain doesn't last forever, the guilt and the shame shall fade away and create a new being within yourself.

As said by Loki, *"The sun will shine on us again."* This collection is concrete proof of healing and deliverance.

Sit back and take it all in because I promise you! There is something in here that will speak to your soul.

Nicole,

I'm very proud of you and continue to shine your light. It's brighter than you think.

•   Angel U. Somarriba

Preface

Many times throughout my twenty years of life I have heard these words said over and over again:

"You are too young to have those kinds of feelings."

Granted, there were times when the phrase had been worded and directed differently. But nonetheless, the implication was one and the same; My feelings were too complex for someone so small, therefore, they were not real.

That mindset irks me to this day. Why should emotion be given a timeline, when it is the very thing that connects us to each other? Makes us *human*. I am not some ticking time bomb, and there is not a poignant doomsday awaiting me at the end of my girlhood. Although, if i'm being honest, I believe girlhood *ended* the day I was told my emotions were not normal and that I felt too much. You would be surprised how quickly a child grows up when they are made to believe that that is the only way they will ever be validated.

All that to say, there will no doubt be those who read these poems and thoughts and think the very same thing. There might even be some who worry, as I understand that there are some things I have penned that could be hard to swallow. Especially by the people who know and love me.

Please know that when I write these tender words it is because I once felt them deeply and vigorously. That regardless of my circumstances now and in the future, they were once *real*. I trap these feelings in paper so that my mind may breathe. So that *I* may breathe. It is only then that I can begin to understand where all this pain and emotion came from in the first place.

And from there, learn how to give it to Jesus and, finally, let it go.

Can You Hear Me Screaming is split up into four portions. The section that might appear the most heavy and unsettling, is the first; *Worn*. However, in truth this section means the most to me because it *is* heartbreaking. Every piece in *Worn* was written during the last two years of my life, aka the most traumatizing two years of my life. Too often we are taught to shove our agony back down our throats so others will not choke on it. But what people, usually the ones who have not experienced this specific kind of pain, fail to realize is sometimes what is discomforting for some is relieving medicine for others.

The reason it was so important to document the dark moments, in detail, through my poetry, and then put it out there for people to read, is because when we write things down we open the opportunity for those feelings to become alive and present for someone else down the road.

When I'm healed, happy and fulfilled in the future and I meet someone who is where I am now, and tell them *"I was in the same boat once"* and they doubt me (as we often tend to do in the midst of pain) there will be physical evidence they can read that shows how I *was* in fact like them. And more importantly, that they *can* in fact come out of the dark hole they are in.

I hope you do not get completely lost in that which is my chaotic mind. But I do hope it touches you, somehow, in a way only words can.

• Nicole E Wicks

Can You Hear Me Screaming?

"Crawl inside this body, find me where I am most ruined - love me there."

– Rune Lazuli

CONTENTS

Worn

Human

Faith

Perceive & Release

Worn

"You're so polite with your sadness. You don't want to ruin this for anyone."

– Silas Denver Melvin

I feel it too

I was thinking today about when people get heart transplants, how even if the procedure is successful the body can still reject the new heart.

I found myself getting annoyed with how singular, stubborn and independent the human body can be.
These doctors have spent hours at school and hours of training so that they can skillfully and carefully give a fading soul another chance at life. And the recipient who's receiving this new heart, probably very much wants to live.

But at the end of the day it's not even up to them.
It's up to if their *body* wants to accept this new heart. It's a matter of if the *body* wants to accept this thing it knows it needs, and is good for it.
I thought about this for a while, how there were probably people out there in the world silently begging their body to just *obey*. And I thought about how angry that made me. I proceeded to sit with that anger for a little, until I realized it was really just zealous compassion.

Because although my heart is not dying,
I know that feeling too.

When your body rejects everything that can make it feel better.
The aching plea to simply be allowed to just live, without the pairing thought of having to survive.
Only in my case, I am both the pleader and the heart.
My own body keeps rejecting me, and I cannot make it stop.

No matter how hard I beg.

I Bite.

I am like a dog that gets backed up into a corner.
I cower or I bite, there is no in between.

Like you, once

Anytime I tell someone my story and where I am now,
I always anticipate the awkward silence that is induced
by not knowing what to say.
Followed by the naive solutions they have to offer for the
situation they will never truly understand.

I simply nod quietly until they've said all they want,
and although I bury my bother as I see
the pity flash across their eyes,
what I really want to do is scream.
I want to shout at them
THAT I WAS NORMAL ONCE TOO!

I swear there was once happiness and life inside me
before my mind tied my will up along with my limbs,
and my body locked me in a cage and strung the key
to the exit door so that I could not reach it.
I PROMISE I WAS LIKE YOU!

before this sickness made me a stranger to the very
thing that makes me human, living.

Unknown absence

When you live with anxiety for so long
it almost becomes like a toxic relationship.
I hate you, *you're killing me.*
But I don't know what life looks like without you,
and that scares me.
How can something so destructive be so familiar
to the point where I'd rather have it eat me
from the inside out, then live with the empty hole
it'll leave behind.

Kindergarten

Does anyone remember those old ropes with the loopholes on the sides our teachers would make us hold onto in kindergarten in order to stay together and make our way through the chaos of the things going on around us?

I feel like I need one of those in my brain.

All I know

I keep telling myself that one day I'll think about anxiety or depression or throwing up and it won't feel as familiar as it does right now.

Right now it's all I know.

In the midst of exhaustion

Why does pushing through, hurt so bad? If this is the price for life, then take it from me. I do not want it.

Anxiety is the predator, I am the prey

"You'll feel better once it's over"

Five words that are meant to comfort,
but instead cause further affliction.

It would seem that way on the outside wouldn't it?
That with pain, relief must eventually follow.

It's like going to a zoo.

It's hard to be scared of predators when they are kept in an
enclosure. It is easier to be brave and think conclusively
when you know that the beast on the other side of the glass
cannot touch you.

For me, I am on the side *with* the beast.
And it senses my every move.

Anxiety is the predator, and I am the prey.
I do not feel relief when it ends, instead I feel disappointed.

Disappointed that dying was only a feeling and not a result.
Not because I want to die, but because living means there is a
probable chance that it will happen once more.

I will have to dance with my predator all over again,
while you stand by and watch.

Battle of the body

I can't remember a time where my heart
wasn't pleading with my mind.

I guess there has always been war inside of me.

Grief

I once heard someone say
"Grief is love with nowhere to go."

In the moment I stayed silent, but in my head I responded.
I am grief.

Grounding

Today my therapist had me practice grounding.
After taking a deep breath, stating today's date
and acknowledging how my body felt,
she asked me a question.
 "If you had to put it into a percent,
how much of you is actually in the room?"
"26%" I said, almost instantly.
Her eyes went wide, and I just laughed.
but it wasn't really funny, was it?
It was just the truth.
I do not feel alive.
In fact, I think I might have died a long time ago.
I want to know where I went.
I want to understand what happened.

Someone, anyone…
help me understand. *Please.*

Trapped

I'm stuck inside a cage, and that cage is my own skin.
It makes me feel uncomfortable…

                        as if it wasn't even mine to begin with.

What about me?

How is it that someone can go through the darkest tunnel in
their life and then move forward like nothing happened?

I see people walk out of these tunnels unscathed and intact,
and I have to ask myself *what did I do wrong?*

Why can't I let it go?
Or push on despite the fact that I want to throw up and scream.

Are they stronger than me?
Or am I just what the monsters love to eat?

Instead of coming out lighter like everyone else,
I seem to collect what they all left behind, when they were
freed.

Is there something wrong with me?
Why is the thing I hate most something I'm afraid to let go of?

*

If you take away the thing that has controlled me for so long,
all that will be left is the distorted person that was once me.

I can't go back to how it was before, so what does that leave?
Would I fill that now empty space, or let it be?

And if it is to remain hollow, will there even be a me?

Concerning love

It is not exhausting to love people,
It is just exhausting to be me.

Smother

I just want to know what it is like to not ache. I am always aching. I am always suffocating myself. And I am tired.

I'm sick.

I'm sick.
It's not a crime, but I feel guilty for it.
I can't control it, but I feel responsible.
I want you to love me despite of it,
but I don't know how to let you in.
I don't feel much anymore, but I cry all the time.
I want a better body, but i think i'd still feel trapped
in a new one.
because it'll always be *me*.
I want you to understand, but I'm too tired to explain.
I want to feel better, but I don't think I even remember what
that looks like.

I'm sick...
Does that scare you?

Diffidence

What if I'm not as strong as you say I am? What do I do then?

Distant rage

I'm so calm with everybody else because I've wasted all my
energy on yelling and being frustrated with *myself.*

Most of the time no situation or thing a person says
can bother me more than how being *myself* bothers me.

So I shrug it off. Because in my mind, compared to how angry
I make *myself,* it is not a big deal.

Landslide

I'm falling into my old habits again.
Will this self destruction ever end?

Or was I always just made to be the example; of what happens
to a person when they lose all their will to try.

The fear of abandonment

It's funny how someone can barely raise their voice to me and
suddenly I'm eight years old again holding back tears,
violently pushing ways I can be better into my mind.

Pleading and praying that this fit of frustration
does not mean they are going to leave me.

Unknowing bliss

how does a person come near me and not
immediately call for help?

can't you hear it?
can't you see it?

I'm being swallowed by my own mind.

Calamitous merit

I will bleed myself dry for you because
I care about you and love you.

But I will also do it because I believe
I deserve to be bled dry.

Even though I do not want it, and even though it hurts,
it is what I think I deserve.

Too much.

There is a terrible, sad groaning creature inside of me
and I cannot let you see her.
I have been told to keep her in, that she does not belong.
And I know if i ever let her out, if you ever see her,
you will confirm what those adults told little
eight year old me.
That I am *too much* for people to handle,
that I am *too much* to love,
that I am *too much* to even acknowledge.
And then I will have to sit with that aching truth,
like I have all my life.
Only now it will be on display,
for everyone I want to want me, to see.

Hurstview

I think part of me stayed behind when I left
my childhood home.

That was six years ago.

Who's going to tell her that we are not coming back?

Why not me?

Even trees get to shed and start over.
Why can't I?

Bothered

I like to act like the things people say to or about me don't
bother or get to me. But the truth is everything gets to me.

I'm *always* bothered.

I am in a constant state of feeling invaded
and defiled by the things around me.

Words fail

People think they want to see you at your worst so that they can love you anyway. But they don't really mean it.

I know they don't. Because I've let people see. They see what that looks like, *what i am*, and any kind of love they have for me gets replaced by fear. They can still like me. But any *love* just becomes *terror* and I cannot just sit here again, fully skinned and displayed in front of someone I am in love with, and watch them become scared of me. I can't. *I won't do it.* So no. It doesn't matter how I feel.

Because no one can know what is happening inside of me.

It's not your fault

I think I'd rather have no one know me than be a burden to people who did nothing wrong, other than knowing me.

Endurance

Sometimes I think if I were to stare at nothing for long
enough, the nothingness would finally swallow me up.
Giving me someplace to go…

Mindlessness does not appease loneliness, and I fear I am
enduring both.

Don't come too close

I'm afraid that if you stay near me, my sadness will
eventually bleed into you.

I would have already left.

I promise you, if I could claw my way out of this body and just move on, I would have done it by now.

Show me how

How do you let go of something that's clinging onto you?

A fool's hope

I hope one day I'll be able to look grief in the eyes
and tell her I moved on.

Then, with relief, turn to guilt and tell him *I won.*

Human

"to love and lose and still be kind"

— Warsan Shire

Human nature

I hate my human nature.
Hate toxicity, yet feel it rise up in my
throat any time I am threatened.
No one will ever know the brutality it took
for me to appear this tender.
My heart wants to show compassion and maturity,
but at the same time my bitter brain
wants to show you how much harder I can hurt you.
I want to be good,
but my dark tendencies would rather be *right*.
So much so that I feel them slithering
up my spine, no doubt on their way
to spew their venom onto my tongue.

I set something in stone then go back
on my word so I can prove to no one
that I can be different if I choose.
I want to be good, but hypocrisy
is in my blood.
I resent the ones who left me to drown
yet when someone makes an innocent mistake,
rather than showing the compassion
I wish someone had shown me,
my first thought is to drag them down with me.

I hate my human nature. *I want to be good.*
I know I am not a monster, but I could be.

Thin

I'm skinny.

I always have been,
some say because of genetics
I always will be.

Because of this great achievement
I'm supposed to be grateful.

Not complain about
the parts of my body
I do not like, because at least
I can see the definition on my stomach.

nevermind the fact
that you can also see my ribs,
for that is clearly not what catches
the eyes of men.

How lucky am I
to have wrists so small
that others can wrap
their whole hands around them.

nevermind the fact
that they shake when i go
to lift a fork because
I feel too unsteady in my own vessel.

*"You'll never understand
your privilege of being able
to eat what you want,*

without worrying about
if you'll get bigger."

nevermind the fact
I've slid down walls
night after night,
because no matter
how much I eat,
my weight keeps going lower and lower.

Yes, I can fit into
the same shirt
I wore when i was 5,
but is no one else concerned
with how long I've been fighting
for the will to survive?

I am constantly struggling
to find the courage to eat,
despite the fact that I love food.

Clearly anorexia means nothing,
when the Lord bore me small.

80-90 pounds at nineteen
isn't detrimental,
if I've always remained below 115.

my deep agony is only
ever really "shallow sorrow"
since there is not enough width
and substance on me
to make room for something more.

the sickness I feel in my belly
is a blessing as long as
the outside remains flat.

and no amount tears
and nights begging God
to make it all stop,

because I can not stand
how uncomfortable my bones
feel against my own skin,

will make others listen,
as long as I am thin.

Complexity is not a sin

To truly appreciate someone is to admit and accept that you will never fully know them.

This need

My body is shaking with the need to be better for you.

No matter how many times you hear me say I hate love
and that I don't want anything to do with it,
please, know that I am lying.

I adore the idea of love so much that it makes me sick,
and I have never wanted someone so bad in my life.

Hungry

We (humans) are devouring each other
with our need to be seen and heard.

We are like a pack of wolves fighting
over the same dead rabbit.

We're all hungry.
yet act as if the others aren't.

So much so that we are willing to rip
at each other's coats to prove that our hunger
is more intense than anyone else's.

But we are all wolves.
And we are all hungry.

Misleading

I wish I had realized sooner that someone saying
"I want to be with you forever"
doesn't always mean the physical version of them.

You will be with me forever, but now, only in my memories.

And because of that, I am sorry to admit that sometimes I wish
we had never met at all.

Longing & contentment

I don't want to be perfect.
And I don't want to wake up as somebody else.
I just want to wake up and like being *me*.

I'm just asking, why?

You love how I make you feel,
but you don't love who I am.

I love you as you are,
but I don't like how you're making me feel.

This is how it's always been.
I just want to know why.

Let me forget.

"Maybe down the road things will work out, and we'll find each other again."

"I hope not." I whisper.

I know you don't want me

Sometimes I think you're meant
to be mine, while other times
I think I only feel that way because
I want to be closer to you.
And the only way to do that,
is by falling in love with you.

I want to know what makes you tick.
I want to understand you
in a way that is so unique
that you can't help but constantly
wonder if this, our connection,
is meant to be something more.
Just as I continue to wonder.

I think you could love me.
Or at least learn to after you
see just how much I can love you.
I know I do not look like the girls
you tend to pine over but
I promise I'd do my best
to portray myself as someone
you could be proud to be with.

I know to the naked eye it
seems like I do not offer much
but I can promise that
I would not break your heart.

I already loved it when it was just
the heart of my friend but now,
it would be so much more.

I know you don't want me to be yours.
But I think we could be extraordinary
if you did.

My love, my life

My love, you are somewhere on this earth.
I haven't met you, but I already hate being away from you.
There is this feeling inside me that I cannot name,
but I know it has to do with you.

What a waste.

I'm sorry that this world made you think
it was a crime to be gentle.

The little girl/boy that resides in you,
did not deserve that.
You did not deserve that.

Sensitivity is not something to be ashamed of,
and innocence is not a sin.
Crying does not make you weak.

And shutting off the emotions God gave you
does not make you strong.

It just dehumanizes you.
And *that* is the true crime.

Sheepskin

People do not like what they don't understand.
It scares them.
Even if the ones they begin to lose understanding over,
are the ones closest to them.

Suddenly, it's as if you were just a wolf
in sheep's clothing all along.

Suddenly you're the problem.
Suddenly, *you're crazy.*

It'll pass.

I love you.

I hope one day I'll be healed enough to tell you that,
without having to worry about the feelings that come after.

Your needs > mine

I think maternal instinct goes wider than our ovaries
when we find someone we would genuinely
put above ourselves.
When we see someone who's inner child needs saving,
and we decide that regardless of the pain
we will have to endure,
we will make sure they have what they need to grow,
and be given a chance to live,
without having to feel like they're begging for it.

I see the hurt that others have carelessly
or maybe even maliciously inflicted upon you,
and suddenly my weak will feels strong,
as if there are two magnets attached
to either end of our souls,
and mine is desperate to get to yours.

My body is no longer my own.
I have you to consider now too,
since you came into my life and consumed
every inch of me.

I will be better for you.
Because I want to, but also because I must.

Foreign space

You are like the cosmos.
You take up so much space yet you are foreign to me.
I have not seen you, but I know
you are breathtaking in every way.
However, I cannot help but fear
that when the time comes,
I will fail to admire you properly.
So I can't help but wonder
if it is not better to just continue
to admire the idea of you, rather than to know you
and let you down.

Howl, if you must.

You screamed and hissed at me to leave,
but when I looked in your eyes
I could see you were scared to be left alone.
So I came closer.
Between every howl and with every step,
your eyes became more comprehensible.
To the point where they were no longer eyes at all.
They were mirrors.
A clear depiction of the little girl trapped inside of *me*.
She wanted to be saved too.
Without thinking I raised my hand,
trapping your cold wet tears between our skin.
For a moment it seemed as though we could meet
each other where the heart meets the mind,
and become each other's home.

But as it is often so, the mind,
despite its need for the heart,
always finds a way to rip it open.
And as I looked down to see your hand
on a knife and a knife in my heart,
I couldn't help but mourn for you.
Even though *I* was the one who was dying.

Who or what was it that turned you so cold?

What color was your skin before the world
sucked the love out of you and left you to wilt?
What could I have done to warm you up,
if I had only arrived in time?

I will carve out my heart with this knife
if you tell me that you want it.
I will gladly give you my skin,
if you say you are tired of being cold.

I will give you my blood if you have bled yourself dry.
And I will stay here with you until my eyes close.

Because I know the feeling of being abandoned.
And that despite how you may scream and scratch,
you do not want to be left *alone.*

Infected

He dismissed my pleads for gentleness
as mere outbreaks, then had the nerve
to itch and complain when
the virus *he* created,
spread from my bones into his own.

Now we are both infected.
Now we must both be cleansed.

Cruel rules

It's hard acknowledging just how many people will only love me, if they can touch me. Maybe I was always made to just be loved *conditionally* by humans.

Maybe unconditional love for me in this cruel world is an exception, and not the rule.

Paradox

The thought of being lonely forever scares me.

But the thought of feeling anything different,
scares me even more.

Can you?

If I tell you my thoughts, will you promise not to use them against me?

Ophthalmophobia

I am afraid that one day you will wake up and see me as the monster you once thought resided in your closet.

Hollow

"I love you." She says.
But not in the way someone wants to be told;
Sweet, gentle and full of hope.
No.

Instead, she says it like how a person
pulls out a knife from their chest:

Knowing it has to come out,
and feeling relief when it does,
but dreading what is bound to come next
as the poison slowly seeps into their blood.

He just sighs.
Walking past her, but stopping just behind.
They remain this way.
Back to back, with only a few inches in between.
Neither one turning to face the other.
The deafening silence ironically
epitomizing what this- *no.*
What *they* have always been.
Hollow and *empty.*

"I love you." She says.
He replies simply. *"I know."*
Turning his head just a-sliver.
A negligent, last attempt to somehow
touch the soul he could never fully reach.
"And I will mourn for you, everyday because of it."

And with that he leaves.
As if he was ever really there to begin with.

This forgetfulness

It grieves me how easily we forget people.
How we can go from picturing our lives with them forever,
to trying to remember the special moments we had with them
months later, when we randomly hear their name.
It makes me wonder if it was all just a waste of time.
Because surely, if it was *true* affection, humans would not
forget so easily the time that was spent with those people.

And the meaning that it held.

A lover's hypothesis

I think love is when you crave silence,
but happily welcome their noise anyway.

Just maybe

I don't believe in other universes,
and I know there is no such thing
as reincarnation.
but if I did, and if there was;

maybe in another universe
I could have been born as
your mother rather than a
mothering figure for you to use.

maybe then I would understand
why you do what you do,
without being angry at you for it.

maybe then you'd love me
unconditionally too.

and I would be able to see myself in you,
instead of seeing what you
ruined in me.

Pomegranate

I wish I had told you nothing about me.

you still wouldn't of cared to know,
but things would have ended with me feeling
a little less exposed.

Choices

The love of a friend takes up one part of the heart
whereas being in love consumes it completely.

I'd much rather have part of my heart ache than all of it.
A human can only take so much.

It's never simple

Wanna know a feeling that sucks?
Knowing that the right choice was made in order
for you to live your happiest life, being content in it,
but also wishing the people involved had just been
better people. So the choice wouldn't have had to be
made in the first place.

An entry I wrote for my future kids

People will not always think the way you do.
Even if they have similar opinions, it is rare,
if you start to look closely enough,
that they think exactly the same even in an agreeing subject.
I think humans need to come to terms with that better.
We are individuals who crave intimacy.
A form of intimacy is the act of being understood.
Even by people we may not like.
But we can not force people to think as we do,
and while I think you should always stand firm in
what you believe in, never bending to peer pressure
or what society expects you to believe,
you should not condemn someone else for thinking differently
about what is right and wrong. *Because to them they are right.*
You can disagree with someone, and still respect them.
Respect doesn't always mean complying with someone's
behavior or morals.

Sometimes respect is just being kind.

Growing cold

You know I love you. But I don't like this version of you.

Come closer

Please,
do not be afraid to reach out
and touch my exposed flesh and bones.

It is simply what I am made of.

It is the inner part of me
that is rarely seen.

I learned to cover it by
sewing together layers of skin
that were more pleasing to the eye.
So that others would not choke
on that which is raw.

But we can only conceal
our insides for so long.

It may look tangled, jagged and red,
but it is still *me*.
It is still *mine*.

even when cut open and
spilled out before you.

Please.
do not be afraid to reach out and touch it.

It is still me,
and i would never
try to hurt you.

Deafening negligence

Sometimes a person's actions are so loud that
I can't hear a word they're saying.

a wrestle with mankind

I think I would have grown up
viewing *men* a lot differently
if I had not come from a womb
in which I was constantly defiled by them.

If I had not been forced
to endure their barbarity,
simply because I was not
capable of screaming "stop".

How am I expected to trust men
when they have been bruising me since conception?

I think as well, I would have grown up
viewing *women* a lot differently
if the one who grew me inside her
would have allowed that womb to *just be mine.*

Instead of forcing me
to share it with men I did not know.
Men whose last thoughts were to be gentle.

How am I expected to trust human beings
when I was exposed to their violence
long before I could meet their eyes?

How am I expected to meet a man's eyes,
with the intent of finding gentleness,
when I've known what lurks behind them since the beginning?

Who will teach me how?

Exposure

As long as I don't allow someone to be
close enough that they can see my flaws,
to me they aren't there and I don't have to face them.

But the unfortunate thing is,
you do not have to give someone permission
in order for them to get close enough
to see those flaws.

Some people don't ask,
and by the time you try to back away, it's too late.
They're already there.

And they can see everything.

Faith

"The fact that our heart yearns for something Earth can't supply is proof that Heaven must be our home."

— C.S. Lewis

Simply Jesus

I never understood why God wanted *me*.
Doesn't He know that my actions are haunting?

Yes, I am the Lord's bride.
Yes, that's what they say,

but if that is the case then I continuously
commit adultery everyday.

Trust me I hate it, I promise I've tried to stop.
But the devils' had this hold on me
that he refuses to drop.

I've cried and I've begged for
him to just set me free,
but then the Lord reminded me
that satan's freedom is *not* what I need.

I need a weapon so strong that
it can break every chain.
A weapon so powerful,
that it can dissipate pain.

I looked up to God and asked what
weapon I needed. He replied;

"Child a mortal weapon won't save you
but Jesus Christ can keep you breathing."

But the moment I heard the only way
was through God's son,
my heart broke in two because I knew,
He'd seen all the unforgiving things that I'd done.

So I cried out
"Lord, please have mercy on my life!"

And Jesus just smiled.
Because all He saw was a blameless wife.

He walked up to me,
put his hand on my face,
and one by one the devil's
chains began to break.

All I had to do was *ask,*
and He instantly set me free.
The son of God just called me *blameless.*

How can this be?

As He began to remove his hand,
I saw that nail driven hole
and it was in that moment
I knew my sins had to go.

So I took my baggage,
along with my worldly deceits
and I bowed down to God,
laying that now old life, at His feet.

To you my life now may seem plain and boring,
but the Lord is leading it.

And his mercy?
It is new every morning.

So the next time someone says;
"Hey, why would you give up your old life?
What are your reasons?"

I will tell them that what I gained was so much better.
And what I gained was simply Jesus.

Partnership

It's ok to need people.
Even God didn't want to be alone.

So He made humans.

Because even Him,
the powerful,
supreme ruler of the world,
knew that a life lived in solitude
isn't a life lived at all.

The art of forgiveness

Pray for them until you're not angry anymore.
Bless them until *you mean it.*

It is only when we give the person who has wronged us,
up to the One who created them,
that we are finally able to move on,
and let our grudges go.

A call for deliverance.

I can't help but feel as though
I am rotting from the inside out.
Lord, reach inside and cut off what is dead.
Bring to life what is still hanging on.
Please.
I am mulch without you.

A dog, and his vomit

I have a bad habit of finding the beauty in dirty things.
Yes, the Lord says come as you are,
but He does not intend for us to stay the same.

Anytime I trip and stumble into mud,
rather than washing myself clean,
I fall in face first.
Succumbing to the sludge.

In my head, if I am covered in dirt
then I cannot be seen.
But my feeble mind forgets that
God does not need eyes to identify me.

He pulls me out and washes me off,
and you'd think after that I'd finally stop.

But I keep diving deep
into that dense deadly mud.
Rather than face my maker,
I always decide to run.

I tell myself it's ok to embrace the dirt.
That this is just me being "honest".

But even then I know the truth.
What I really am is a dog,
who keeps returning to its own vomit.

He understands

Sometimes I have to remind myself
that Jesus was afraid to die too.

Precious

what you did hurt me
to the point where I could not stand.
my chest felt on fire,
and no matter how hard I clutched it
that pain would not die out.

It was the moment when everything
stopped and my body went numb
that I made my declaration.

i am done!
i refuse to show anyone
any part of me again!

not when all they do is
tell me I'm no good,
then smear my body with gasoline
and light a match that obliterates the
gentle flame that rests in my tender bones.

i will bury my love deep inside of me!
i can be cruel too!

but then Jesus whispered to me;
"That is not how I made you."

it is not your fault they were not ready to love you.
it is not a crime to crave the same love that you give.
they were not ready to nurture your fragile heart, but i will
tend to your precious wounds until somebody worthy is.

In my weakness I fell back to my knees
but this time there was someone to hold me.
and while I laid there and wept,
my declaration shifted.

I will not harden this
fragile heart.

i will not turn cruel!
there is still love inside of me!
i will remain gentle!

these wounds will turn into scars
and once they do i will be ready
to try again!

but I will not repeat,
and I will not forget.

Jesus says i'm too precious
to settle for less than what i give.

Returning to Eden

The story of Eden is truly heartbreaking.

Perfect untouched creations
betraying their maker
simply because they
did not understand the
importance of saying "no".

I can't help but wonder
how the Lord felt when
He clothed Adam and Eve.

The agony He must have experienced
from having to cover up something
He created to be pure.
All because they chose instead,
to uncover the things that would only bring destruction.

He knew one could not exist with the other,
without eventually bringing about chaos.

He could have stopped it then and there,
left them naked and ashamed,
returned them to the dust and started all over.

But he did not.
He loved them too much.

When He looked into their eyes
He saw you and me and knew
He could not bare to be without us
let alone lock us in a cage,
simply so that we would obey.

He wanted us to choose Him.

Because after all,
a will is not truly a will
if freedom is not attached to it.

So He let them live.
Knowing one day
He would send His Son to die.

So that down the road,
when the time was right,
we could all be together again.

Returning to Eden,
living together, once again uncovered,
the way God had originally intended.

An ally

Nothing upsets me more than when I hear people say
"God does not care about woman"
Or that He is prejudiced towards them.

As if it wasn't God who removed a man's rib
and declared that without a *woman* by his side,
he would not know balance.

As if it wasn't God who chose a *woman* to
save a nation.

As if it wasn't God who sent His Son
through a *woman's* womb.

As if it wasn't God who instructed Jesus
to have the *woman* at the well be the one
to spread the word that our Savior had come.

As if it was not Him who scolded men
when they prepared to stone a *woman*
for an offense she did, in fact, commit.

As if it was not Him who then proceeded
to help this *woman* up,
and call her blameless.

What is a more beautiful act of love towards women
than to let one be the first to tell the news
of Jesus' resurrection in a world full of misogyny.

God is not the sexist one, people are.

Molded Destiny

It is evident by the way my vessel responds
to the Word of the Lord,
that I was created by God himself.

It makes perfect sense,
what better place to find shelter
than in the mold from which
you were shaped in.

A baby clings to its mother
because she is all they know.
And as they grow, regardless of if they
have shifted apart from her,
there will always be a pit in their stomach
that longs to be near her once more.
Because they were originally formed
and dwelled within her.

The same goes for Jesus.
The world can pull me away from him
but He will always be imprinted in my spine.
For it is known,

an artist places his mark on his work.
I am the product of the Alpha and the Omega.
His Word is the proof of my origin,
a destiny that is bound to be fulfilled.

I was made to be a child of God.

When did you know?

Sometimes I wonder what age it was
when Jesus became conscious of who He was,
and what He'd have to do.

We learn from the Bible that even as a boy
He knew the temple was his Fathers house.

Did He know then, as a child,
that one day He'd have die?

I wonder if He became a carpenter
so He could become familiar
with this mixture He would one day be bound to.

So that when He hung on that cross,
He'd have something to distract Him
from the smell of His own open flesh;
the memory of just being a boy, in his fathers workshop.

I wonder, as He hung there to die for me,
if there was a split second when He thought to himself

*"I wish I had stayed inside my mother's womb just a little
longer"*

As I often think.

Or even then, in Mary's stomach,
did He have the consciousness
that His first breath in this world,
would begin the journey
that would lead to His last?

Regardless, He came out of her and into the world anyway.

I hope one day, I can be that brave.

A love note to creation

The truth is I used to be afraid of it.
of all the chaos that comes with the Earth.

But now, it seems to be
the only kind of chaos I can bear.

It is my escape.
and it gives me peace,
to be enwrapped in it.

To know that I am amongst
the very thing my body
will one day return to.

When my spirit has finally
made its way back to Heaven.

I am grateful for the Earth.
Thank you Lord, for giving it to me.

Little white boat

When I was little the Lord handed me
a little white wooden boat.
This boat had been made when I was born,
but I was finally old enough to acknowledge it.

It was perfectly crafted, no mistakes.
And the moment I took it into my hands
I knew it was meant for me.

The problem with humans and precious things though,
is that the longer we have them,
the more familiar they become,
and the more familiar they become,
the less precious they appear to us.
Even though the value of it is still the same,
if not greater.

There were times where I'd be careless with my boat
and accidentally leave a scratch.
when I did, I'd take it to Jesus immediately,
feeling overcome by guilt.

"I'm sorry." I'd say,
"I put a mark on my gift."

Jesus would smile, gently replying with
"It's ok, we'll fix it together."

But as I got older scratches turned into nicks
and those nicks made cracks,
and next thing I knew I was 20 years old
and my boat had snapped in half.

I knew the best thing to do
was to bring it back to its maker.

But every time I'd head towards His door,
Lucifer would give me glue
and tell me to put myself back together.

I did what he said because his method was quicker.
That, and I was ashamed to face
the man who had acquired splinters
on behalf of a gift I had now tainted.
So I continued to use this glue.

But what happens when the glue runs out?

When the one who tricked you
into using it in the first place,
then uses this temporary solution against you?

Who now will fix my boat?

I can't climb in it and hold it together,
my weight is too heavy
and at this rate I'll drown.

Well, the truth is I've been drowning already.
There's only one person who can help me now.

I assumed He'd send me away
before I'd even have a chance to reach the door
But not only did he welcome me,
His welcome was *warm.*

He asked me if there was anything I needed,
and in less than a second I fell to the floor,
utterly defeated.

I pulled out my once white boat.
Only now it was a dirty brown,
broken and beaten.

Refusing to meet his gaze,
I muffled through sobs.
"I'm sorry. I'm so sorry."

"For what my child?" He asked softly.

Confusion coursed through me.
"I ruined your gift!"
There was no reply.

*"You worked till your hands were bloody,
and I threw it around like it meant nothing."*

*"I know I have no right to ask for your help,
I know you've probably given up on me, but it hurts."*
I choked out.

"Could you please do something?"

As I awaited His answer,
I couldn't help but sputter out
a handful of sorry's.

I was silenced by the feeling
Of Jesus' hand on my head.

He crouched down to meet me where I was.
He was smiling, looking at me intently,
with eyes as gentle as ever.

"I forgive you, It's okay."
My face scrunched up in disbelief.
He moved his hand to my shoulder,
and engulfed me in a hug.

"How about we fix it together?"

Jesus placed half of my boat into His right hand
while I held onto the other.

He gestured for us to put them together.

And as i watched my boat
return to the color white,
and saw the two once broken pieces restored to one…
I knew; I was home.

And that I would never trade my priceless boat,
for something so shallow and fleeting, again.

Judas

I once heard a pastor say

"The Lord allows us to be betrayed because
He wants to see if we can learn to forgive our Judas."

But if that is the case,
I am Judas.

I need to learn to forgive myself.

For all the times I traded in
the Bread of Life for something that was deadly,
and not meant for me to consume.

It was there

I never really understood how peace and love
could concord with each other,
until the moment when Jesus knelt down,
met me where I was,
and put His palm to mine.

Suddenly my hands were just hands,
rather than knives.
And the gashes and blood I had inflicted upon myself
were washed away with His own.

It was there, where His flesh met mine, that the scales fell.

It was there that I learned that peace and love
could not only exist together, but be one.

It was there that I learned
what it *truly* meant to be human.

An excerpt from my personal journal:
regarding humanity and Heaven

{March 31st, 2024}

There is a tight ache that rises in my throat when I read the word "human". Just now, I read it in a devotional and I had to stop because I started to cry. I think it hurts my heart to know we could have all escaped our own self destruction, if we had just chosen God from the beginning.

I also think when I hear this word, I am enveloped by this concurrent cognizance of what *makes* us human.
And it overwhelms me.

What of this nature is God given? What of this nature is not? Are the things I find beautiful about humanity things God instilled in me, or am I blindly admiring my own self sabotage?

To feel and think this deeply, about just being, is something only humans can do. Without Jesus, we are doomed.
Yet angels still lean in when they hear us cry out. They have tasted and seen righteousness first hand yet humanity still mesmerizes them. And the reason for this is because they cannot worship God as we can. Because they are celestial, and we are human. I find this to be beautiful.

[I also think I know the reason as to why I am so easily brought to tears over this word.] I think I cry when I hear the word "human" because this life is the only time we truly get to be.

And half the time, we are doing it all wrong.

Perceive & Release

"I hope that someday when I am gone, someone somewhere picks my soul up off of these pages and thinks, "I would have loved her"."

— Nicole Lyons

Scales

I stayed because I caught glimpses
of your kindness and I wanted you to be better.

I wanted you to be better because
that would've meant that you wanted to change for me.

But all this did was distract me from the root problem;
that you were not good, and that you never once thought
something was wrong in the first place.

A poem for one of my best friends

I hope you know I'd die for you.

Grab hot coals with my bare hands,
if it meant keeping you warm.

Become a monster if it meant
keeping you gentle.

I'd dull every knife in this world
with my own skin,
if it meant you'd stop carving out
your delicate beauty in order to
appease that devil on your shoulder,
that has made you believe you need to be different.

That has tricked you into seeing yourself
as something other than serene.

You look as though the earth chose
to mold itself *after* you.

The rivers echo the smooth dip
that your curves encapsulate.
The rain falls according to your fervor,
so that even your tears won't
have to know what it's like to fall alone.

The grass compulsively works
with the rain and the soil,
so that it might remain
the same color of your eyes.

The very eyes that make me
feel seen, and safe.

The eyes that have been blinded
by her father's incontinence,
and tainted by man's
inability to treasure gold
for what it truly is; *priceless and rare.*

When I think about how
the world has disserviced you,
I cannot help but think of the blind man
who Jesus healed.

Simply by rewiring his DNA
with the very substance of which he came from.

Please know love,
if I had the power,
I would take my own handful of dirt
and glide it gently over your eyes.

In the hopes that you
would open them and finally see
that it was not you who needed
to adapt, but them.

It was not *you* who needed to carve.
It is not you who needs to change.

You are perfect, just as you are.

Absolved

I cannot appease that of whom
expects every inch of my soul, but gives back nothing.

not nothing in return, *just nothing.*

The importance of submission

The most powerful and beautiful things, that are created to be fulfilling and pure, oftentimes can be the most dangerous and harmful to your heart, when you do not submit it to God first.

Materialistic

I wish you were as generous
with your love as you are
with your money,
when it came to me.
Or maybe I am just expecting too much.

Maybe you swiping your credit card
is just a silent metaphor
that I, the little girl who
only ever wanted your attention,
am too afraid to acknowledge.

That this is the only way you *can* love.
Materialistically, and with limits.

It's a complex

You can understand and still say no.

Remiss

I wish younger me got to see this version of you
instead of the one that warped and ruined her idea of love.

Oh well.

To the ones who stayed.

How do you repay unconditional love
when all you've ever thought you deserved
was conditional tolerance?

I promise that I will spend
the rest of my life trying to
give back the same amount of kindness
that you've given to me.

Because of you,
I finally understand,
aside from family,
what *real* love is supposed to look like.

It is apparent to me now, that not all family is blood.

You made me see that.
Thank you.

The rant my birth father will never hear:

Just because you dipped out early
doesn't mean I noticed it late.

It wasn't
"oh he must of had a good reason,
thank God he didn't stick around
then abandon me when I was older."

No. You know what It was?

It was
"How could he hate me already?
I'm only eight, what did I do wrong?"

Kids aren't clueless, they just get confused.
Especially when a person they trust
leaves before explaining why.

So don't say you love me
and that it was *so* hard to let me go.

Because If it *was* that hard,
and you *did* love me,
then you wouldn't have done it.

Want it back

It's true, adulthood is special,
but being young is *precious*.

Never take it for granted.

It's ok.

You will never be able to make them understand.
Just let it go.

Be better, please.

I cannot forget the past.

Not. when. you. keep. repeating. it.

Hypocrisy is a disease

You can carry bitterness on
the strength of good intentions.

But it doesn't make you any less bitter,
and it doesn't make it any less wrong.

Self inflicted

Sometimes I reflect back on how much I tolerated from a person and I can't help but think to myself;

"What were you thinking?"

We have to mean it.

Changing for the better doesn't always come with a reward.
Especially not if it isn't sincere.

Candie

I think the times I feel my birth mom the most
are the times when I am in a heavy state of anger...

I feel her a lot.

> *This has to change.*
> *I have to change.*
> *For the both of us.*

Unrequited effort

I've always wondered what would happen
if I just stopped being the one who apologizes first.

Specifically for things that weren't even my fault.

Butterfly Effect

Ignorance is not always bliss.
Sometimes it's just ignorance.
and sometimes one persons bliss,
is the expense of another's life.

we have to be careful.

It's simple.

Treat others the way you wish they treated you.

No more conforming

It is not my job to make sense to you.

Disservice

To invalidate my pain is to invalidate your own.

Pinky promise

I don't think I will ever fully get it right,
but one of these days I promise
I'll start getting it right more often.

I will change for the better.

And yet, I must.

Somehow I must learn to accept things
as they are rather than
how I wanted them to be.

No matter how bad I wanted it.

A goodbye to my childhood

{8-31-23}

Dear youth,
I used to tell myself
that I wanted to leave you behind.

That being older meant being seen,
and the independence that came with it
would replace the loneliness I felt as a child.
But I was wrong.

The truth is now that I'm here,
one day away from finally saying
goodbye to my childhood,
I find myself clinging onto you for dear life.

Begging you to stay a little longer,
and regretting all the times I pushed you away,
in an attempt to fit in with the older crowd.

I wish they would have told me.
Told me that I didn't need to grow up sooner,
or try to act older.

Surely they must have known I'd regret it later.

Instead, they commended and praised me,
as if it was a triumph to be so mature
at such a young age.

I hope my last attempts to
reach out to you will be enough
for you to forgive me
for how much I took you for granted.

That, when I step over into adulthood,
you will still come to visit me from time to time.

Reassuring and reminding me
that the little girl I once was
did not have to die in order
for me to become the woman
everyone expects me to be now.

I hope you will not try to leave me
like I tried to leave you.

I know it is selfish to say that but,
even now as I enter my 20s,
I simply cannot bear to be left alone.

Thank you for everything.

Sincerely,
The little girl who grew up.

Epiphany

I am learning that the most
fulfilling form of love,
is to love and be loved.

I love others to the point
where I bleed myself dry for them.

But I also think I deserve
to be bled dry.

To the point that when people
offer up some blood of their own,
so that I might not collapse,
I turn them down.

As if I do not need it to survive.

It is in my self reflection
that I am coming to the understanding
that I will never be able
to know and feel the fullness of true love,
to love and be loved,
if I continue to hate myself
more than I love others.

Sanguine

A lot has changed,
yet simultaneously,
nothing's gone back to normal.

I'll never be the old me again,
but I'm not helpless anymore either.

I am not better yet,
but at least now, I have hope.

It'll be ok.

"All lights turned off can be turned on."

– Noah Kahan

Acknowledgements

I first want to give thanks and glory to my savior Jesus Christ. Anything about me that might be perceived or acknowledged as a gift is from Him and only Him. I would not be alive if He hadn't laid His life down for me. So thank you, Lord. For chasing after me every time I felt unfit to be your daughter, and for reassuring me that there is a reason I am meant to, not only be alive but, *live*. Thank you Zion, my cover artist, but first and foremost one of my best friends, for taking time to create that which cannot be expressed through words. You made my vision come to life, and I am in a constant state of admiration when it comes to your talent. To you, and to my other loves, Cait, Ayva, Ireland and Sophia: Thank you for showing me what it means to be loved and known by people who have no obligation to know and love me. Each one of you encapsulates the beauty of John 15:13, and because of you I understand its meaning. Although I will never understand what I did to deserve your sisterhood, I promise to cherish it forever. Thank you Angel, for writing such a moving forward. You have encouraged me to write my story since we first became friends, and I cannot help but feel honored that you would say such kind things about me. You will always be one of my inspirations when it comes to telling a tale, whether it is fiction or nonfiction. And last but never least, thank you mom and dad. You two have chosen me since the beginning. You've shown up to every recital, every show. Held me through every triumph and every heartbreak. Supported me every time my goals changed, and kept me alive when I no longer saw the point. And not once have you, two people who did not intend to adopt a baby in your fifties, complained. Thank you daddy, for always taking the time to listen to my work even though you don't always understand it. Your intentionality means more to me than you'll ever know. Thank you mommy, for inspiring me and showing me how transformative the world of writing can really be. I know I cried and fought with you as a kid, wondering why you wanted me, a ten year old, to learn highschool level reading and writing at my age. But now, I could not be more grateful. It is because of the two of you that I even have a story to tell. So thank you truly, from the bottom of my heart, for everything.